THE LITTLE BOOK OF
CAT
PHRENOLOGY

T0364028

CONTENTS

CRAWL INTO THE SOFA · SQUEEZE IN
LL SPACES · BEWARE PLASTIC BAG ·
TT · IGNORE · STRETCH · WALK AWA
BELLY · 'T RUB BELLY! OUT
, BE IN TE
· VO MI
N! · CA N B
OCK T RO
E HOU E
AIN · E
O SMA
LICK
AY ·
SIDE
E D
ON
OC

UNDERSTANDING YOUR CAT

Do you ever wonder what goes on inside your cat's head? Like why doesn't he seem to care that he's blocking foot traffic? And why does she cuddle with you on some days, but on other days give you the death stare? When he watches you expressionlessly, is he silently judging you or contemplating his next snooze?

Essentially, your cat is an enigma wrapped in a mystery.

The wheels that turn inside a cat's head have always fascinated us. There are many different opinions about a cat's thought process, especially when it comes to our very own little furballs. Sometimes you'll hear the overly simplified explanation, "Cats only have three things on their mind: food, sleep, and litter box." (Of course, the person saying this almost always doesn't have cats or is the person in the household to whom the cat pays zero attention.) Then there are the rest of us who believe that there is so much more that goes into a cat's intelligence. Because your cat's perpetual pooping in the bathtub has got to be some sort of cryptic message she's trying to send you, right?

PHRENOLOGY: A MINI HISTORY

If we were to look to the popular pseudo-science from the 19th and 20th centuries, we might be able to find answers to these puzzling questions.

Phrenology was an early form of psychology that was believed to offer knowledge into human behavior. A Viennese doctor, Franz Joseph Gall (1758–1828) thought that the ridges and indentations in a person's skull could give some insight into their personal traits. Doctors like Gall mapped out sections on a model's brain and designated them with aspects of personality traits, called faculties, and used those models to explain why someone behaved the way he or she did. The sections were used by doctors to measure a person's behavior, labeling them with things like "love and feelings toward others" ("amativeness"), "greed" ("acquisitiveness"), "love of excess" ("ideality"), "individuality," and "self-esteem."

CAT PHRENOLOGY

·····◆·····

So what if we were take the same principals and apply them to cats? It is safe to say that we could uncover some thought-provoking information and even explain some of the mysteries behind feline behavior.

The cat head bust that you have here will be your guide to understanding everything you've ever questioned about your cat's peculiarities. Our study of the feline brain identified several behavioral categories that are found in most cats: Food, Resistance, Indifference, Conflicting Behaviors, Vengeance, Calculation, Helpfulness, and Quirkiness. Sections have been labeled on the bust from each category, so you can see where some of your cat's behavioral faculties are located.

Keep in mind, none of this has been scientifically proven.

FOOD

• • • • • ◆ • • • • •

We can agree that a cat's priority, first and foremost, is food. Not only does is a cat probably thinking about food at any given moment, but you've probably noticed that your cat has several unique ways of getting you to feed him or her *right this second*. Here are a few sections that pinpoint a feline's desire to eat whenever it's convenient for them:

RESISTANCE

•••••◆•••••

It's no secret that cats will not do a single thing that we want them to. This can be anything from not coming to us when we call them to the downright "absolutely not" terrain of not coming out from under the bed in order to avoid us shoving medicine down their hatch. Here are some high-frequency sections of resistance in a cat's brain:

CRAWL INTO
THE SOFA

SQUEEZE INTO
SMALL SPACES

BITE

INDIFFERENCE

•••••◆•••••

You may have noticed your cat's severe lack of interest. Got a brand-new toy for her? *Yawn*. State-of-the-art cat tree all set up for Fluffy? *Sniff* and walk away. A cat's feeling of indifference is all too common, but the next time you spot one of these behaviors, you'll know not to take it too personally.

CONFLICTING BEHAVIORS

∙∙∙∙∙◆∙∙∙∙∙

Does your cat's behavior seem to mean something one minute, but then the complete opposite the next? You're not alone. Cats may seem like they've made up their mind, but it is best not to assume this. Here are some common mixed cat-messages that we find in a feline brain:

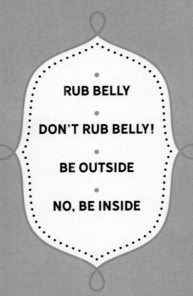

RUB BELLY

DON'T RUB BELLY!

BE OUTSIDE

NO, BE INSIDE

VENGEANCE

•••••◆•••••

As cat parents, you are probably all too aware of a cat's natural desire to express their displeasure at us and other pets. Sometimes you might not even be sure what has gotten your cat into such a peevish mood, but chances are you've suffered because of it. These sections represent only a few of the behaviors that a cat will use to settle the score:

CLAW FURNITURE

TEASE DOG

VOMIT ON FLOOR

WORLD DOMINATION!

CALCULATION

••••◆••••

Cats have the amazing ability to stay laser focused on their prey—or a dust particle floating by. They can display intense behaviors that are not only very entertaining to watch, but also indicative of how cats perceive the world around them. Here's what goes off in the feline brain when they have spotted a moving target:

CHASE

STALK

POUNCE

BIRD!

HELPFULNESS

◆ ● ● ● ● ● ◆ ● ● ● ● ●

Surprisingly, cats do have a desire
to be helpful. It's true. However,
what a cat may think is helpful may
not always translate perfectly in the
human world. But before you scold
Fluffy for delivering a dead mouse to
your bed, maybe this will help clear
up what *he* thinks is helpful.

**LOUNGE ON
KEYBOARD**

**SIT ON IMPORTANT
PAPERS**

**POOP OUTSIDE
OF LITTER BOX**

**CHASE INVISIBLE
OBJECTS**

QUIRKINESS

There is no denying that every cat has a distinct personality. Cats sometimes do things that leave you scratching your head in total confusion (Why does he love to watch you in bathroom?), but their strange behavior is just another reason why you love them. The following behaviors are just a few of the many quirks that are located in the feline brain:

**CATERWAUL
AT 3 A.M.**

SIT IN BOX

**KNOCK THINGS
OFF TABLE**

**DART AROUND
THE HOUSE**

FOR THE LOVE OF
CATS

◆

There's no question that we love
our cats. Despite their quirky
behaviors, at the end of the day we
wouldn't trade them for anything.
It's impossible to stay mad at them
for too long when we catch them
climbing up the curtains or knock-
ing things over, because it's only

a matter of time before they will be purring in our faces and acting adorable. We may not entirely know what our cats are thinking or what drives them to behave the way they do, but, hopefully, the *Phrenology*

Cat kit has given you a few ideas as to why your furry friend does what he or she does. So the next time you catch your cat meowing in the shower again, remember to check the cat brain!

This book has been bound using handcraft methods and Smyth-sewn to ensure durability.

••••• ◆ •••••

Written by Marlo Scrimizzi.

••••• ◆ •••••

Designed by Susan Van Horn.